Eternal

Essays from Afar

Expressive Press © 2021

Contents

Introduction

In the beginning there was rock. Then came water.
Water revealed the *skin* of the mountain. Then came the stream,
river, loch and sea. Then came the forests, woodlands and flowers.
And then came the animals and then ourselves. Wilderness had
arrived once again. Of course, all of this happened *through* the last Ice
Age. Instead of a beginning and an end, life was recreated,
rejuvenated. All came again for us to see, witness and admire –
eternally. Everything within nature *is* eternal. Eternal in expression
(appearance and function), *essence*. Measuring the very beginning of
our planet Earth is therefore not so important, what really matters is
the *presence* of our living planet in the here and now. For example,
the quality of the presence of mountains testifies to the deep and
complex relationship between their form and their essential role in
our hydrological system. The presence of a skyscraper cannot offer
the same quality of experience as a mountain.

Life, therefore, is a story without end, and this makes me begin to
think about my own arrival in Killin and the time I have spent here so
far. I have lived in the village for over four years – not a long time for
us humans. But when I begin to think about that space of time in
terms of experience, it feels much longer. One might therefore be
more daring and suggest that I have lived in the village for over 400
years (at least that is how it has felt at times), when I compare my
experience to the age of the mountains surrounding me right now –
over 500 million years old. I realise with each passing day how unique
and rare it is to live in a mountain village and therefore experience
the deep time of our living souls within us; which is eternal. The time
of mountain formation had contributed to the realisation of this
process. In all of this, what I am talking about is the very *quality* of life
itself, what one can experience in the presence of nature on a daily
basis. With the mountains, I was able to experience for the first time
in my life the weight and depth of my own soul; the deeper our

connection with nature, the deeper our experience of life and therefore its richness and true meaning – our destiny.

Living in this mountain village, I have felt and still feel a natural continuity of time living beside nature. A time that is *outside* modern time, today's digital clocks and watches. Occasionally, but not all the time, the tyranny of our current socio-economic model can interrupt the flow – the flow of the seasons, for example – and then I have to find a way back into them, grounded. But when the interruption occurs, suddenly, survival takes precedence. It is survival without sense – man-made, often unsustainable (therefore unethical), reflecting the poverty of life that has *not* been created by nature herself. Monopoly of our common land is a modern example of our deprivations. Let us therefore continue to keep putting nature first at the heart of our daily *being*, so we can bring about a new culture and the birth of the human economy.

From Afar: Ontology of a Mountain Village

I don't think there is anything left to experience in our cities today, other than endless consumption and the illusion of infinite choice. Whether in relationships or careers, we still consider that the city represents real progress in life. But the city can never give the same quality of life that nature can give us; when you love a city, it is rarely reciprocated. Take, for example, our mental health and wellbeing – nature is strongly recommended as the cure, the healer, by our doctors (they never advise you to go shopping). This is why we should adopt the ontology (defined as the quality or essence of existence[1]) of a mountain village as a model for a more ethical way of being. For example, when people come to visit Killin, often they report feeling 'tired' much sooner than they would normally when living in a city or town. This tiredness occurs because our bodies are being forced to slow down and live in accord with the rhythms of nature – at first, it all feels scary.

We are not sure if we can trust the spiritual quality of what we are experiencing right now in the presence of nature through our senses because we have adapted our bodies to survive in busy and stressful environments. Furthermore, the better the quality of our experience of nature, the greater the ebb and flow (gravity) of time appears and therefore the more difficult it is to overcome the force of nature and resist her natural rhythms. Even if we succeed, to do so on a permanent basis is impossible (often we have to give in). When we leave the presence of nature, we take with us an experience that adjusts our bodies to a pace of life that is more natural and attuned to our needs – it is not long before we plan our next trip. Therefore, the experience of visiting and living here in Killin gives us nothing less than what is essential to our *living* selves. It provides the option of improving our quality of life by putting nature first, at the heart of our local economies. It is possible to live an eternal life now rather than thinking that such a *way of being* awaits us only after death.

In a mountain landscape such as Breadalbane, one is more aware of living on a planet, than in a town or city today. In a city, nature has no permanent presence, we encounter it only occasionally here or there. All that is left during a full day in a city is the sky – an eternal sky. That might be the only hope for city dwellers nowadays. They look for a cloud in the morning, afternoon and evening (any shape is welcomed), birds, anything that is of nature; the sky of a city is probably the only direct experience of nature that *cannot* be controlled or destroyed by man. However, with climate change city skies may become greyer, giving us more reasons to leave and begin a new way of being *elsewhere*. It is without surprise that the essence of living in a city is therefore *limited* to what we consume, and the people we expect to meet along our journey. Essentially, therefore, village life offers a more ethical way of being and gives deeper meaning to our existence than a city can ever offer. The writer John

Berger said the following about the importance of a centre, a human home:
The point about centre, it's where life naturally makes some sense. Home is the centre of the world because it's like a cross, there's a vertical line and there's a horizontal line and along those two lines come the following, the horizontal line is all the roads leading out from the village, from that centre, across to other places and finally to all over the world. It's the way you get to that home, on the surface of the earth and then there is the vertical line, and that is where the dead and maybe the unborn, go up and down between earth and heaven, and when they cross like that, that is a place which is really home, because the dead and your ancestors are there in the cemetery, the children who are married and will have little children, or perhaps still be there and then there is all the traffic in the world and when you live in a situation like that, the question of answering, why are we here? A question of finding sense is much easier to answer but in how many places in the world is that now true, either large cities or villages in fact in very few.

Sanctuaries

Between the rocks and water one can *place* one's soul; a sanctuary has been found. When walking, one can do that. Sanctified. Walking *through*, *with*, *behind* and *around* the mountains of Breadalbane, one can therefore always find places of rest; inspiration and rejuvenation. It is not long before one begins to feel one's essence is restored; it is not long before one begins to feel content with one's life again. You see, living in a space like the mountain village of Killin, one of the most profound things I have come to know is how one can think of it as only a small place. One has got to know it quickly ('nothing much to see here') and yet there is a surprise around every corner. For example, I am still meeting new people from the village after four years. It is as though the unique space of a mountain village preserves or keeps people a secret: when they are ready to reveal themselves, the time is right for them, they come out from behind the mountains. It is the same with the mountains themselves: there are secrets waiting to be rediscovered through them, you, us. There are infinite sanctuaries to be rediscovered daily here in this landscape of Breadalbane, in a matter of minutes, not hours – all is there for you. Therefore, in this book, *Essays from Afar,* I present to you something of my own journey so far – my experience of nature along the way, my own philosophy of nature and life itself. For example, I include my thoughts on the deserted village of Tirai; climbing my first mountain (Meall nan Tarmachan); experiencing rock art – cup and ring marks – for the first time–; my thoughts on ecotourism; meeting with and discussing the photographs of Richard Phillips, a local wildlife photographer; climate change; a meditation on walking, and my experience of smelling an apple tree in bloom. All of these aim to look closer at our relationship with nature and how that can be refined on a daily basis as we live out our lives.

[1] Throughout this book, I define 'ontology' less in terms of the investigation of our being, and more in terms of the essence of our being. The more of our essence we reveal, the more we exist. Only our experience of nature can help us achieve a real quality of life (one that is at least sustainable) as we attempt to move away from a consumer-based ontology and today's global socio-economic model.

Breadalbane: Home of Giants

'Taileachd said to Fionn, "I would leap the channel backwards, and unless you do the same, I shall have the fame by right."' – *In Famed Breadalbane*, William Alexander Gillies.

In folklore, Scottish warrior Taileachd and Irish warrior Fionn mac Cumhaill battled against one another to prove their might and worth for a local 'lady' who they both loved. But how did this fight between them begin? Well, the challenge which led to both warriors becoming giants was set by the lady herself – "I will make order for you, and be not angry with each other. The man who wins the victory in a leap, it is he that I will follow with pleasure." And so, the warriors 'went out' amongst islands, lochs and mountains and leapt. What is intriguing about this story is how the woman wanted these men to be giants, and the men had to learn how to become giants. What these stories represent is the relationship between our imagination and natural landscape. Without the mountains, there would be no giants, no legends, no heroes like Rob Roy MacGregor. They also represent a sense of continuity as we strive towards unity with nature in our daily lives. History, I believe, is a form of travel. We can use it in times of need to replenish our souls, for example, and as a way of seeing, where we might need to take a few steps back, or forward – like giants, the day of our embrace with the world in which we live shall come. Each and every one of us is a living monument, our relationships with nature and with each other are therefore unique.

Forgotten Village of Tirai (Glen Lochay)

On maps today, these ruins are simply known as shielings. Without roofs, they can't be considered as bothies either. A shieling is defined as '*a mountain hut used as a shelter by shepherds*', or from another perspective, '*a summer pasture in the mountains*'. In our culture a 'hut' would be considered a 'man-cave'. These are the ruins of a village, however. When you encounter such a place, you can sense that is has been a village and all you can do is wonder what happened to reduce it to a shieling. How did this highland village become deserted? Was it abandoned? If so, then why?

In the precise moment when the inhabitants had to leave their homes and animals, how did they feel? How long had they lived there? Did they have children? You see, when you begin to look at their homes, like I am now, you crucially realise that their stories are invisible to us, out of sight. This is fundamentally about the intrinsic values of village life, before anything else.

Instead, their stories are preserved around the stones of each wall they had built. How? Because they are still standing – shouldn't that be enough? Something of the village has survived and we must try not to ignore its existence – we must try to preserve its history in respect of the lives that once lived here. The walls of their homes are still standing. They have not fallen yet, nor are they in total ruin. This little civilisation was their life. This was how they sustained the land, animals and themselves – what freedom! It is not surprising that the Gaelic name given to the village – Tirai – means 'land of joy'.

Knowing their stories would mean living there, spending time sitting next to their homes, looking at how each home nestles into the landscape – measuring with your eyes, the walls of their homes with the mountains surrounding them, or how they used standing stones to become the central focal point of the village. Looking and listening, one can begin to see their stories unfold. Becoming intimate with the landscape is essential to knowing their struggles and joys. It's about going deeper. How did they live their lives?

How happy were they? How did they see life? How did they see their future? What would their reaction be if they were to see the world as it is today? Most importantly, would they have been satisfied with the quality of their lives, – would it have met their needs? In the modern world, the quality of a person's life is often measured by their mortality. But the actual quality of life in terms of experience and fulfilment may vary whether or not you have lived a short or a long life. And yes, essentially what I am stating is that the only way to measure the quality of a life is through people's *experience*. Therefore, what was their daily experience of life? How good was it when compared to the way we live today?

Land is a place where our waking dreams are realised, where they begin and end. New settlements begin on open ground bringing the opportunity for new expressions of gratitude (from life being a gift). Therefore, representing a way of being in the world. *Living*.

The village may be deserted today, but we must remember that the original Inhabitants would not have abandoned their village without solid reasons. From the research I have done so far, a census of 1871 recorded that 'no one' remained 'living in Tirai'. And there are no other records of life existing there after that date. Tirai had come to an end. If we go back to trace the beginning of Tirai, the earliest and at present only record we have is the village being mentioned 'in 1451 in the Exchequer Rolls of Scotland', meaning that Tirai had lasted as a village for 420 years up until 1871. I believe, however, that the village is much older. One can only imagine the culture (let alone the stories) stored up and passed on to generation after generation – where are they now?

In 1797 It was stated that 'there are eleven families on the farm' and that was 'considered to be too many'. Yet, they had each other, there was the family unit, and the village itself, a family – not made up of separated fragments, like today, with individuals being forced to become single units. It seems, from historical facts, that the collapse of the village was a gradual process - as opposed to a sudden, single event or crisis. Therefore, the end of Tirai, I believe, would have been made up of a series of critical events that would have led to its eventual collapse. An example of a critical event was 'in 1807 farming became difficult with tenants unable to meet their rents'. Big landowners, with a desire to increase their profits, once again forced the tenants to abandon their livelihoods and their lives for the sake of profit. Our current attitude to land ownership and the use of land remains the same.

The people of Tirai, therefore, did not abandon their village, they were forced to do so. The decision to abandon their village was not theirs – they could have continued to sustain their lives there by subsistence farming. The decision was a political one on the part of the landowners. The villagers were no longer considered profitable, because they could not meet the 'increase in rents', and yet as a village they had managed to survive for over four centuries. What the village of Tirai exemplifies is the effect of the profit motive which is in itself unsustainable, and persistently pushes out the needs of others. Where something is gained, elsewhere something is most definitely lost. In a new economic exchange without a profit, Tirai, when we consider its *economic* energy in the 420 years of its existence, would have been able to sustain itself and critically its culture too for well over 1,000 years.

Roles within the village were many – shepherd, ploughman, tack (carpenter), miller, general labourer, housekeeper and servant. Some of the inhabitants had to leave the village to earn a living as some of these job titles suggest. But before this transition, self-sufficient crofters were persistent in finding ways in which they could carve out their independent way of life in and around the village. How amazing would it be if we could begin the process of weaving together ancient and modern roles of being in the world today? Wouldn't that be more modern?

There was also a lime kiln based in the village of Tirai, which we could consider part of a micro green industrial revolution. Can you believe it, Tirai was already being Modern and revolutionary, in the sense that the villagers managed economic survival through their existing connection with nature, knowing that they could transform Glen Lochay into something of a serious commercial limestone quarry. Their little lime kiln suggests that they had no desire to exploit nature, only to sustain and make the most of what resources they had available to them. Most certainly, there was no corporate dream as we see today.

Imagine if the village of Tirai could once again be brought back to life, becoming a Highland eco-village using renewable energy and sustainable agriculture methods. Isn't that how life is supposed to be – made for living, not just existing?

Standing as I often do in the village of Tirai, I see in my imagination the villagers sitting quietly, looking out towards mountain and sky, feeling and knowing through their senses the true meaning of life. Dreaming far and wide as they did, through the glen, past lochs, across oceans into the universe, and beyond...

Becoming your Landscape

It takes a long time to become your surrounding landscape. Some landscapes are *chosen* by you, some *find* you, many we are *born* into … and some of us seek *new* ones. The more you know your landscape, how it came to be as it is today and what changes are happening now, the better you can know yourself. But to do that, you have to know a little history. You've got to have a strong desire to go further, searching far and wide, and as deep as possible. Once you've explored your landscape, which may take many years, what will you become, what will you be?

A Mosaic Dream: Meall nan Tarmachan

Morning. I am standing at the bottom of an entire massif that stretches in between me, eternally. Why have we humans separated mountain into mountains through names? We know there is only one, we know they are all connected. I am now about to climb mountain. Not far from where I am standing is a loch created over time since the last Ice Age. And beside me as I'm walking, a mixed woodland of species tangled like a labyrinth.

In order to get here, I have walked through a village that is surrounded and shielded by this mountain range. Everywhere, as far as the eye can see, draws you in. Towards the mountain's textured and overlapping peaks, each peak offering you a pillow on which to lay your head. Cushioned clouds enwrap themselves around each snowy peak.

I feel my body to be barely awake, as I begin following a man-made track, leading me, I hope, to a summit. I am walking steadily through a coniferous plantation, a few birch trees appearing around each bend. I feel tired, unmotivated and stop quickly to refuel, sitting on a large rock. Between the straight-lined planted conifers, I notice small streams pushing themselves through the gaps, as they continue travelling down towards the loch. And what about the infinity of these rocks? Often, they are carried and begin their journeys in streams from the top of a mountain, and where then will they go? What new destination awaits them? Everything in nature is a continuous rejuvenating process in which to support life *eternally*.

On reaching what I thought to be the summit, I find to my surprise that the summit was much further away. I quickly realise that my perspective looking at the mountain from the village is completely different to that when you enter *into* mountain. Distance, it appears, when looking, can never reveal how far one actually has to walk from the ground because of all the things you discover about the nature of the mountain.

The further up I go, the skin of the mountain is continuously being revealed to me, forever changing in shape and pattern. In front of me is a long ascending hill of grazing pasture, sheep with their lambs are visible in every direction. Sheep or rock? One has to look twice to confirm the answer. I then look behind me and find without surprise a messy plantation. Conifers ready to fall off the cliff edge alongside the many dried-up stumps. I climb over a tall fence, designed to stop deer jumping over into wilderness. Each mountain has its own name, including the name of the ridge – why isn't one name enough? I head towards the unknown.

Beneath my feet the earth is dry and brittle. There is too much grazing here and very little of the original flora and fauna that once lived here, wiped out to make way for today's sheep that have no real market value. I'm now looking at a crack within the earth. I arrive at what is called, in geological terms, a youthful stream. I want to bathe and become it. I also discover it has a name, stream *Gypsy*. I edge closer to its eternal sound.

I look into the stream in search of its beginning. I step *into* stream.

>Standing now in stream

>eroded rocks

>in the shape of *steps*

>skeletal structures of animals

>elevated

transcended

jewelled remains of an ancient palace

not a man-made palace

nature's house

(*mica schist*)

(*silicon* and *oxygen*)

(*muscovite*)

glassy lustre.

My mind is as clear as the water I'm now looking into ... rocks, pebbles and sediment. Where is this stream taking me? It's only silver that shines from the rocks but it reveals infinite surfaces. I imagine that on the day of our unity with nature, our bodies, mind and spirit will be of this colour.

Transparent.

Lucent as the flowing stream beside me. Pushing ahead, I follow stream all the way to the top of mountain. The higher up I go through the spring snowfall, the more I feel I am approaching *dream*. And the more I keep walking through the melody of the snow fall, again the more I feel I am being transcended further. Again, the colour of our unity with nature – the eternity of our body, mind and spirit – will be of everything we have *seen* ... as I slowly now become stream. Then I see looking through stream, not just the surface of rocks from which we came but profoundly I am also seeing the very surface of the human skin, the *imprint* of our souls.

From here, dream reveals to me the first humans pressing their entire bodies within water against rock, which was soft and fresh, a skin out of which they emerged new as the youthful stream I am in. Before he and she came out from the stream, as their bodies began to outgrow the embrace of the rock, slowly they moved, only a few centimetres up and down. And from the imprint of their souls, as they continued to swim between the bedrock and the thin surface line of the water, exploring between the two, *emerged* a body.

Moving their bodies (scraping against rock), their skin renewed itself from the old rock they no longer resided in – just like the tiny tadpoles swimming around them. And like the frog spawn, our birth began as human *amphibians*. I now begin to understand the imagination of Kingsley and what a 'water baby' is. Slowly opening their eyes whilst lying on the bedrock, they looked through the moving water and saw a blue sky. Bubbles of oxygen began to rise from their mouths, each one bursting into atmosphere. Then as they began to lift their bodies, they felt for the first time their own body weight; gravity had to be immediately overcome. Raising their entire bodies at the same time; neck, legs, feet and arms; taking their heads above the surface of the water, and there a human face appeared, *expressionless*. Each breath becoming a wonder of pleasure. He and she stood fresh from the water, side by side. It was from the stream we came and shall return.

What I was seeing that day was a mosaic fusion: between our biological being and spiritual *becoming*.

I was closer to both the pleasure of what dream and dreaming actually is - the dynamism of dream. I was inside the dream of our creation. The dream received that day was being shared with me from elsewhere. And importantly it revealed to me something about the timescale within the act of creating. For when we dream awake, and enter into the place of dream and begin to imagine (for dreaming is creating) the moment is *without* time. What you have created can immediately be seen within your imagination. Motion within dream is without constraint (for the relationship between what one is imagining and feeling within such a moment is reciprocal).

Understanding this reciprocal relationship cannot be measured with today's human instruments – it can only be measured from the pleasures we feel through the senses. This is essential if we want to get closer to the aesthetic value of our waking dreams and to judge precisely their authentic meaning before making them reality. This can only be achieved if we learn to distinguish the difference between the significance of transient and eternal pleasure. The lasting pleasure I experienced from this waking dream was testament to its authenticity. There was nothing transient about the experience.

The sensation I felt that day was eternal *in* pleasure, a moment that became and remained eternal; out measuring that of human time. I was eternal. And within that eternal moment, life had intrinsically outstripped human mortality. I was being pulled in and attached to an aspect of life that I had never experienced. What I'm sharing here is not a vision. I'm sharing dream, dream being action within creation. Here among stream Gypsy, I realised that the act of dreaming awake through the human senses is essential to our becoming our own desired creation. Therefore, our waking dreams and the places in which we dream are real, significant and hold meaning rather than just something we imagined. Our waking dreams are essential to our being in the world.

With human time evaporated from my mind and still feeling eternal, I make it almost to the top. I am nearly 1044 metres above sea level. Space, I notice, has become more intimate, as though one has entered into the *rooms* of a house, our bedrooms. Everything feels pure and of virtue. Then I become aware of the silence. I can no longer trace, or see the stream's beginning. I can no longer hear flowing water, only the slow sound of dripping water. This sound and the silence surrounding each drop begins to absorb me. Nothing else distracts my attention; I am free from today's artificial and impersonal interactions. I stand completely still; I can see nothing, only hear what I am now *becoming*...

Earth, water and air.

Becoming elements that make up minerals that make up rocks, from the stream in which our bodies were made. Becoming the mountain's atmosphere, the elements (rain, wind, snow and fog) that surround me which I am breathing in, seeing, hearing, almost touching, and feeling. Becoming the entire stream that reaches all the way down the mountain to the river into loch. Up here, all elements are *intimately* themselves. They are eternal in essence hence why they cannot be broken down into 'simpler' substances. I become everything through the senses within a *single* moment.

I am for an eternal moment part of the universe and am once again reunited. Becoming my essential part within nature. I feel like a Palaeolithic man, reborn. Free in exchange with the universe in which I was created. Everywhere amongst the silence I am in, I feel the tender presence of something already known to us.

Because this experience was completely new for me, I was unsure what I had experienced; I had no prior knowledge with which to define the moment. I felt fear and pleasure. It was a reawakening of my senses. It was a spiritual experience which we find difficult to recognise today and distinguish from our daily activities. We have become blind, blind to the possibility of a spiritual presence in our daily lives – at least to recognising a spiritual quality in our living present (in climbing a mountain, for example). We have forgotten how to live. How to make such moments more a part of our lives. Nor do we know what a spiritual experience actually is. A spiritual experience is more than just a moment; it is an act of unity within our relationship to life, to nature. We have stopped the search for these precise eternal moments that can lead us to a better, more ethical way of being. All our energy instead heads relentlessly in the opposite direction and therefore we miss such moments, moments which contribute to the meaning and quality of our life.

What hasn't left me since that day when I climbed mountain is the profound fact that the nearer I was to the top, the more I became a child. At nearly 1044 metres in the air I was no longer an adult. Mountain is the preserver of childhood. And what the mountain taught me was how to be a child in the world again.

Part I: Cup and Ring Marks – Why Not Sun and Ring Marks?

It's quite confusing at first when you hear or read the term "cup and ring marks" to describe an art form comprising rock carvings from 4,500 years ago. I think it was lazy of art historians (and academics) to call them cup and ring marks. Why? Because it lacks imagination. Why not "sun and ring marks" instead? It would make a lot more sense. It was too easy to say "cup" and "ring" when the time came for them to be named. Furthermore, it is to blur this precious and unique art into something of a novelty. And, also not to appreciate the delicate transition between the Palaeolithic and Neolithic periods. For example, how can we know for sure that 'cups' were actually used during this period? If so, that would mean a lot of cups having to be placed onto one rock (let alone the weight of them to create such markings). The functional implication in the name 'cup' marks is misleading and takes us away from the imaginative quality of the art which is why I think sun marks would be a better term.

No unity has been given, no collaboration, between one sees and the name given to these so-called marks. Rather, the term "marks" is to instil the notion, that they were made by mistake (uncoordinated), rather than through the intrinsic human need to *express*. It also takes away a sense of discovery at the time they were made. Hence, why I think they still remain a mystery. Hundreds, maybe thousands of theories to explain the unexplainable. But are they really that difficult to decipher, understand? They are not codes, why then the persistent mystery given to them? What about the significance of the rock itself? Shouldn't that be included within these masterpieces? Rock for them, was essentially their canvas. Or possibly if not, what about the uniqueness and beauty of how the artist combined sculpture and carving into *one*?

If you look at the photograph, you can see that it looks to be something of a step, hence why this particular rock may have been chosen. Not just because of its natural elevation, but most definitely because of its shape. If this rock was to be dug out, and placed in a museum today, stood up, it's meaning would be lost.

For me, the rings are traces. Traces of something that has either been seen, or possibly imagined, or both. What then did they see? I think they are closer to the representation of a *sun dog*, a bright spot that appears in the sky on either side of the sun. Seeing a sun dog would have been a powerful moment, and would have evoked a conscious relationship between what was happening in the natural world and the feelings of pleasure experienced from such a surprise. It would have been a moment of genuine unity between being and becoming. They are a message of hope. Once again, to name them cup marks is immediately to *reduce* these carvings to something functional and therefore diminish their aesthetic value also, leaving everything else to remain a relentless mystery, rather than reflecting their true meaning.

What if the carvings also represent the rippling effect created by rain drops?

The intricate (and intimate) beauty of these carvings, whether on a summer or winter's day, is a real joy to look at. What this art and the rock on which it is inscribed represents is an *expression of gratitude*. Gratitude for the fact of how beautiful life is, and most importantly to affirm that life is a gift. The human need to have our chosen expression of gratitude realised in the here and *now* is fundamental to our existence. Realised in the sense that it must be seen by others, and consciously (therefore publicly) confirmed as an *eternal expression*. Eternal to what, you might now think? To nature, for everything in nature (in form and appearance) is in essence already eternal. Therefore, I think today we can say and confirm that this art form was (and still is) an expression made eternal, and that the artist had fulfilled what they set out to achieve. How? Well, first their gratitude has survived long enough for us to still see the rock carvings today. And second, the carvings have retained their unique beauty, and critically, authenticity in that they still hold meaning for us today. Those facts alone explain why they continue to intrigue us, regardless of how many mysteries we continue to conjure upon them.

Seeing them is important, because we each bear witness, and thus contribute not only to the quality of our lives (in that precise moment) but essentially to our becoming. What these carvings also represent is that the creators existed (without names), through the tracing out of their existence, for us to admire and love. Their traces also represent their waking dreams and the early days of human civilisation which is still evolving and yet to be fully realised in all its colour. Therefore, I think it is critical that we try not to see such art as having come to an end, from the moment it was made, and the artist passed away. Their carvings are still becoming – the artwork and the rock it is carved from are living pieces of art as erosion and climate continually change them from the artist's original dream. Once again, we must learn how to show real love for these carvings by showing them more attention. Only then will we truly know their full meaning.

Part II: Cup and Ring Marks – The Beginning of a Japanese Stone Garden?

Art is often a way of translating human experience, akin to understanding the nature of something – its essence. Art is also often the desire to replicate what one has *seen*. Cup and ring marks therefore exemplify the human desire to capture the essence, the nature of what they had seen in rock as a record. Recreating that moment takes real effort, evoking the same *unity* in pleasure that men and women felt that day is a real privilege for us.

Recently, I have been paying a lot of attention to the site of the cup and ring marks in Glen Lochay, the rocks and carvings, including the rocks without carvings, for they too, I believe, will have some form of meaning. The site of these cup and ring marks is something of a world in itself. One rock I saw became a mountain. A delicate and intricate world of nature's eternal essence – in all forms, whether rock, flower or mountain. An essence that can never be surpassed until humanity places nature at the heart of our local economies – only then we can begin to live life to its full potential.

Sometimes, when I was there, looking at the rocks, I sensed that a lot of water had once flowed here. Equally, having spent a few days away from the site, that possibly it may have been a garden. Sometimes, it feels like one has stepped into a Japanese stone garden, for example. It's also worthwhile remembering when looking at cup and ring marks that although they appear static (inanimate within the rock) they are in fact a record of something in motion. They are a serious attempt to replicate the aesthetic value of natural appearances, with the aim of getting as close as possible to their meaning; their carvings were a way of *translating* the language of natural appearances.

Ready for Wilderness

Each day when we walk out of our doors into open air, we are preparing for wilderness once again. Each step, walking old and new paths, becoming a dialogue of thoughts, in our daily interaction with nature.

Wildlife Photographer - Richard Phillips

I met up with local wildlife photographer Richard Phillips, who had an incredible range of photographs that represent the rich flora and fauna of Breadalbane. I was amazed at how in the short time he has lived in Killin (just over a year) he has already managed to capture so much. The photographs presented here are chosen carefully to represent not only bio-diversity, but often the unconscious artistic process that underlies taking photographs which we discover when out in wilderness.

Red Stag photograph taken at Glen Lochay near Easter Tullich.

Beaver at work, photograph taken near Loch Tay. Below: *Bullfinch* bird eggs, photograph taken at Glen Lochay.

Common Buzzard photograph taken at Glen Lochay standing on a Utility pole. Below: *Golden-ringed Dragonfly* photograph taken at Glen Lochay.

Red Fox photograph taken at Glen Lochay. Below: *Oystercatchers,* photograph taken at Glen Lochay.

Rediscover Your Connection With Nature Through Ecotourism

First, what is ecotourism? Before anything else, it represents the human need to travel. We'll never stop doing so because it's an intrinsic part of our being. We love to explore and discover what might be new to us, whether it be the known, unknown or rediscovered. It is that great sense of being awakened – we all need that too. The International Ecotourism Society defines ecotourism as "responsible travel to natural areas that conserves the environment, sustains the well-being of the local people, and involves interpretation and education" (TIES, 2015). Ecotourism, therefore, is a global ethical statement. It is a way of embracing both climate change and the human ontological crisis at the same time (one dictionary defines *ontological* as 'relating to the branch of metaphysics dealing with the nature of being'). Ecotourism is about recognising that we have lots of needs as humans, but so does the living planet which we inhabit. Fundamentally, it is about putting nature first at the heart of our local economy.

Scotland, and particularly Perthshire, is an ideal destination for ecotourism thanks to its natural beauty, biodiversity, accessible wilderness and fascinating local history. A major aspect of ecotourism is inspiring those people from all over the world that come to visit Perthshire's local landscapes to find a renewed appreciation of nature: rather than the dogmatic perspective of seeing nature at our disposal and as a thing to exploit for our needs, it helps bring us to the full realisation of our own part in looking after our surroundings. Crucially, it is about remembering that nature supports all forms of life, each life being essential to the other.

It was last year when I decided to start my own ecotour guide business, Eternal Mountain. The idea came after a move to Inverness didn't turn out so well. Although I knew nothing about ecotourism at the time, when I came back to Killin (which is where I now live) I felt that this mountain landscape needed me, that I was now seeing the village with new eyes, even that I had abandoned this landscape but it had not abandoned me – I owed a certain gratitude to the mountains. Being an artist and writer, I saw walking as a real and genuine way of embracing climate change with a new narrative. Subconsciously, I knew that the relationship between the human imagination and our natural landscapes was, and still is, essential to that process of changing how we live today. Local history is in many ways, therefore, sacred – evidence of our past relationship with nature. But we must keep it going.

For locals, part of this ethical statement about putting nature first at the heart of our local economy creates the opportunity for more ethical job roles within our communities, jobs that are low-carbon and less damaging to our planet. This, I believe, is the future of humanity, and it represents the serious need for a universal basic income for everyone. It is also about remembering that a connection with nature has the power to transform and transcend our lives daily, bringing back meaning, identity, function and so much more. We can establish a loving connection with nature – one that is reciprocal and therefore life-enhancing. Putting nature first will contribute to the quality of our lives. We are now beginning to awaken to the revolutionary idea that it is possible to measure and create an economy that is based on the well-being of every human being, as well as nature. Another important aspect, if we are to take on the task of putting nature first, will be to give us the opportunity to redefine our present culture. Most of our culture today is still based upon our current socio-economic model, with the result that we have become too dependent upon a consumer-based ontology which is made up of artificial interactions, rather than natural ones.

Eco-tourism is a way of embracing the challenge of today's human ontological crisis, but only if we are prepared to put nature first, experiencing it in a richer and deeper way. Our history can truly ground us, keeping the human imagination alive and well and helping us to look towards a future with continued and renewed hope.

Climate Change: Creativity and Survival

John Berger, the art critic, once said in a TV interview:

> This creativity, which we are so attracted by in artists, which basically is why we are so interested in artists, this creativity, which in fact is potentially in everybody, *will find it's expression in life itself*. I see art as we understand it as a tragic phenomenon.

John Berger Talks to James Mossman – 1970.

Climate change. We see, touch, taste, smell and hear about it every day. Mostly through media platforms. But we also know of its biological and spiritual consequence through our daily lives. Will our sense and realisation of being in the world ever change? We know, for example, that our present world economy is unethical and unsustainable in every way imaginable.

We also know and can testify many of the effects of climate change through our senses. Our towns and cities are not a 'pretty' sight. We don't interact as much as we used to, spending more of our time looking at screens, and with COVID-19 we're living in an increasingly 'touch free' world.

We are out of reach, 'out of touch' with reality itself and ourselves. What we eat doesn't taste as good as it once did, food is often tasteless and expensive – when was the last time we could all afford to cook a healthy meal?

Oxygen. We are often 'rushed off our feet' through the absurdity of living under the intense pressure of an economy based on survival only. We are persistently 'out of breath.' And we hear, practically almost 24 hours a day on the news and on social media that our existence is at stake.

We seriously have to begin the process of dreaming up an entirely new way of being in the world and that can only begin by using the uniqueness of our imaginations. But firstly, we have to ask ourselves as artists or creatives some probing questions. What is it I am creating right now? And then, what is my aim, goal and purpose here in this moment?

For example, look at the ink drawing on the next page that I did a few years ago. It is a cluster of sloe berries. I want you to imagine these sloes through your senses: what do you see, touch, smell and taste? And then also imagine the drawing itself, which although separate from nature, is still representative and therefore reciprocal.

How would these sloes contribute to the quality of your life? Imagine the impact of the drawing you have just made being shared as a gift to your fellow friends. Think and imagine how such acts would make you, us, feel in pleasure.

If we are to move away from a consumer-based society and to slow down climate change then we need creativity. Creativity is a real and genuine way forward. But it's also important that we recognise and make the distinction in our minds between the nature of creativity itself, which although connected, is still a separate process from the nature of our finished art piece. The question is, which one are we most concerned with today?

Is it the act of creativity or what we are actually creating? If we are not concerned with both of these aspects, art loses its meaning. How aware are we as artists of this dilemma?

When I Walk: Meall Dhuin Croisg

Here, I am – in the flesh.

When we see rocks, we are seeing the time of our creation ... still in continuation.

When I see mountains, I am reminded, 'I know no other shape'.

Tell me, what is the scent of wilderness? Once found, how would you know?

At the top of Meall Dhuin Croisg...

I imagined (or did I see?) myself, a muscular and strong being, alive during the Roman Empire of rule. I saw, as I looked across boulders from peak to peak through Glen Lochay (with the black density of rock) *filling* my mind, a sense of human history as vast and as infinite as the landscape before me. A world, a planet, alive once again. I saw the infinite stretch of the human imagination; the wind pressing hard against my face and body. What was I? Who was I?

Not all that I saw could be captured, remembered. It was a moment, I had only a moment.

What would it have meant to have *lived* during the Roman Empire? A world of meaningless, unjust and untold violence, a life of endless escape routes. How free were you? How free could you *be*? Life would have been hardcore, pain like no other. How would the voiceless or under-represented (the underground, the peasants) have suffered? Those that suffered would have experienced the same kind of pain we experience today. The experience of pain hasn't changed (and will never change) but the type of pain and *way* we experience it depends on forces external to us – it remains political. Today, we experience pain, desperately in despair, alone. What kind of a paraphrase could encapsulate this image of humanity as *we* are today?

When I walk alone there is this inner hope and dream that with each step, we *all* walk together.

There is no getting away. Where ever you are.

They find you. Who is "they"? Find out.

Was I a Roman solider escaping to the Highlands, untouched, unnoticed? Or a giant (peasant) attempting to escape the tyranny of Roman rule (which is no different from the tyranny of today's global corporate elite)? Did I travel alone? Or was it the 'voiceless' travelling as far as these mountains I am now standing upon? Or was I an unknown citizen, fleeing for my life? Was I more a gladiator, than giant? Or was I a legion commander, peering over these Highland mountains, in search of new land, a boundary for the Roman Empire?

What was I *being* hurtled towards? Did it have something to do with the collective human shadow? Our dark side? What darkness was I seeing? Or, was I seeing something from the past return in the here and now?

Is what we see happening in the world today a déjà vu from our past? Close to that of the Chinese philosophical cosmos of 'absence' as a void of 'nonbeing' in experience. Rather than a 'presence' in the world again. Is that what the world is now becoming, or is coming next? An existential crisis (rather than ontological) without being. What is missing? What is the ontological experience of non-being? Mountain tops may at times have harsh conditions, but look at our conditions on the ground, across the globe – life is better in the air today.

Where are the 'ten thousand living things' in the world today? We are certainly aware of the fact that we are getting closer to a planet of 'non-living things'.

Being at the top (I noticed I was present with myself), again the wind pressing against my body and face, with the sheer darkness of the rocks (millions and millions of years old, why not new?) I was able to see them and look at them within a moment. What does this tell us?

Was I seeing something of the tyranny (from the past still present) that was heading my, *our* way? Did I see what I had to become, or once was? Overcoming persistent government austerity and socio-economic oppression has certainly not gone away. And now we have the Coronavirus pandemic. What new exploitation will sweep across the globe this century?

Our negative shadow is the political tyrant.

What I realised in this still barren landscape is that I was standing in the shadow of humanity, a fusion of the personal and collective. Why was I given access to the human collective of our psyche in that moment? How significant was this moment, this connection with our past?

When I walk, I'm walking (subconsciously) or striving towards a point of unity within myself. Biological and spiritual unity of being in the world, a presence. My presence has now given birth, or has it been reborn?

Walking is a free act. When you start to walk, you immediately become your own agent, independent – free-standing, as it were. You are not reliant on anybody. You can act out your own need to be in unity with yourself and the world without co-dependency during a time of personal crisis, for example.

When I walk, I keep walking until I have reached a point of unity. Unity, restored between the lithosphere and biosphere surrounding me, and now within the biological and spiritual sphere within me.

Is the shape of a mountain representative of its ontology?
There is more than one way to feel eternal. The shape of a mountain, of course, is essential to the ontological sphere within you, us and the mountain. Ethics and aesthetics go together – 'True to form'.

Think for a moment – the colours we see from natural appearances throughout a day. How are they contributing to the quality of your life? What can we learn from the presence of nature?

When I walk, often alone (not through choice), there is this hope that *we* all walk together.

I bend with the mountain, or rather the mountain bends me, as I follow its shape. Or, is it actually shaping me? I can never shape the mountain – I can only offer the mountain my love through all of my senses in gratitude.

Mountain is shaping me into what? Does it matter? Let my destiny remain forever unknown, a mystery. Mountain is shaping my body (muscles like boulders), mind and a spirit, once again connected with Mother Nature.

When I walk, I move the mountains and they me. Always moving me first, they moved me from the start, from birth. And yes, they are 'moving'. What do they move us into?

You see, you have to see it from a perspective of ontology, the very quality of your life to appreciate the essence of nature in experience. Measure first how and what you feel. You know and feel yourself to be eternal, however brief or sometimes long the pleasure feels. But what you are made to feel living in our Western part of the world today through all of its corruption, represents and demands a human ethic, a new way of being.

Second, what you are feeling right now, in your being in the world, feels good and right in the presence of nature. It's no longer about place, but space. It's more than clarity, it's a connection most definitely and therefore you feel connected. And it is also a kind of placing. Your whole mind, body and spirit has been placed and therefore has entered into a way of being. Almost like a bubble of oxygen, clear with no pollution, purity. A kind of sphere, like the ozone layer. You have entered into an essence, an eternal way of being, the essence of your being in the world, a planet in which you not only exist, but feel alive.

The meaning of your existence has more power, energy, imagination and most importantly hope, hope, being a life with a destiny, rather than our present culture of doom. And that is exactly what makes walking with mountains so beautiful.

At a point of wave, slopes descend, a fast-approaching ascent. Following the mountain's curves, bends and infinite horizons. I am at one with myself and the mountains. I'm all waves. Curves or slopes? Why not waves? For this mountain was once under sea, a bed. I gently lay myself spread open wide, upon its skin, pastures of not only green, rainbows of colour seen and unforeseen.

Sunlight, bouncing from one peak to another. Shining upon me as I continue to walk. Walking where? Where am I taking me? Or rather where is the mountain taking me? The love of repetition and rhythm.

'Are you going to Glen Lyon?' a stranger asked me. I replied, 'No, just up the road', and we laughed. Undulation?

The sun is my compass. Light sometimes, shining in all directions. I follow the clouds too, their shapes. I yearn to get closer. When I've arrived (got closer to them), there is a new shape, or my looking has lost focus and something else has captured my imagination. I am forever in and out of all that surrounds me. I am looking, looking and looking. I don't stop. I love to look. Often, there is much to see when walking, alongside new perspectives that are right in front of you. But sometimes you don't see anything and you miss perspectives. Then one day you return to look again and then you see something in the landscape, a perspective of looking at the world has been revealed and you have learnt something new about yourself. This is actually a special moment, a gift from our inner world.

Everything I *decide* to become is an act of love. I become only what I feel to be intrinsic to nature, myself and you. There is no boundary, it is without limit.

Maybe my looking is in the search for a seeing. New perception now seen. In what way will this new perception change the ontology of my being? And now becoming ... In what way have I changed within this single day, hour, minute or second? Will I, or have I seen the world afresh again? Or is it another wonderful chance to learn something new about myself? Is it that great chance to reconsider, examine my own skin?

When I look at my body, the first thing I like to touch and feel is my stomach. On my stomach is my birth mark just to the left. Is my birth mark the place that I am searching for as I walk across these mountains?

I know deep down, I've started to realise and learn (almost sub-consciously until today), that I crave or perhaps desire my own skin to match that of this mountain, to be of this eternal mountain.

We can learn all there is to know about reality through mountain. Rise and fall. Birth and death. I want to be as strong as this mountain.

I want to be as strong as the rocks that hold it together. I want my legs once again to become the boulders I pass daily. I can move them with my mind, never my arms. Am I becoming a giant, or a wolf? Or both? I said once to a group of people from the village, 'this landscape does not move fast enough for me'. They smiled and laughed. They knew it didn't move fast enough for them either.

All this change we must do, work, working on ourselves. Why so? First, living at peace with ourselves is paramount. For we live with ourselves every day and before anybody else. Second, so that we can love others better and provide a presence in the world that gives hope. One of imagination.

I am grateful for water and rocks.

Beating of my mind.

Surface.

When I walk, I move the mountains and they me, at a point of waves. Or through waves. I see only waves. In this glen, I am surrounded by waves. Are they really rolling? Rocks maybe, but the massif itself is like a giant wave. Infinite flow. If we are to accept the ongoing absurdity of Darwin's theory of evolution, I was swimming around this area (500 million years ago) as a single cell, still invisible as we are today to the 'naked human eye'. I'm laughing as much as these 'rolling hills', because I could not see myself then, I didn't know that I would begin my life as a single organism, once again as a cell.

That's the unimaginative and biological aspect of my life out of the way: there is still a huge part of our story missing. What about my soul, the 'spirit' part of me? Why isn't that included? Am I just mind and body only? Can there not be another part, making three parts to my existence? I mean, come on, so much of what surrounds us, the meta-physical part of our planet, world and universe is invisible, who are we to say what does exist or doesn't?

When I walk... are we closer to walking together?

Let the body speak.

When we walk, or when I walk, I let my body speak. Speak to the world, surrounding landscape. Let it be known you are here.

Allow, and watch the full unity of your spirit, body and mind come together in full force. Active, alive. Notice the full intelligence in you, notice what you have and can become. Notice the communication between all three, connected. What new destiny are you now seeking? Where are you leading yourself? What new destination is awaiting? And now notice the knowledge of yourself. Intelligence which from our beginning was made to bring all three together.

Evolution through natural selection ... If I keep reading this sentence, then I will understand it. Darwin's theory and the way it is still discussed today is all flesh, constantly observing the changes in our biology and yet never in our behaviour.

Why does Darwin continue to return in conversation, in our written narratives? He returns alongside his theory because of the connection between his theory and the ruling-class, both during his time and today, as part of their ruling ideology (often to justify the existence of their own ruling calculated economic exchange of a profit). Will it ever go away? Neo-liberalism and Darwinism seem to go hand in hand. His theory has seeped into every aspect of our present socio-economic model. This is even more evident with the pursuit of 'herd immunity' in light of the Coronavirus outbreak. The

BBC, for example, strongly represent through their often-biased demeanour and organisational structure the whole domination of a theory that hasn't been entirely proven right for over a hundred years later.

Here I am - in the flesh, here we are – in the flesh.

When we see rocks, we are seeing the time of our creation ... still in continuation.

When I see mountains, I am reminded, 'I know no other shape'.

Tell me, what is the scent of wilderness? Once found, how would I know?

When I walk alone ... there is this inner hope and dream within me, that with each step, *we* all walk together.

Postscript

During the final writing of this meditation, I began to think about and therefore question how far the Roman Empire actually reached in Scotland. I discovered that the Roman Empire never reached as far as the Highlands, instead, the Antonine Wall was constructed around 140 CE, running 60 kms from modern Old Kilpatrick on the north side of the River Clyde to Bo'ness on the Firth of Forth. For a generation it was the furthest north-western frontier of the Roman Empire. But why did the Romans decide to abandon the Highlands (and in fact the whole of Scotland) in their quest for rule?

I learnt the following from *The History and Legacy of Ancient Rome's Northernmost Campaigns,* Charles Rivers Editors, 2020.

> Scotland (known as Caledonia to the Romans) was never fully conquered or incorporated into the Roman Empire. While the Romans made several efforts to subdue Scotland, it is not entirely clear whether their failure to complete the subjugation of the northern part of the British Isles was due to the ferocity of the Caledonian/Pictish tribesmen or whether the Romans simply came to the conclusion that the region had far too little to offer in the way of resources (either minerals, metals, or slaves) to warrant repeated major campaigns.

> Scotland in the 1st century CE had no settlements of any size, so profitable trade was not easy to establish, and so, did not offer any major motivation for military conquest. A further disincentive to any Roman general looking to achieve a decisive or speedy military victory was the terrain. Unlike much of England which, although forested, was relatively flat and so allowed for roads to be built, Scotland was both wooded and mountainous. Scotland today, as then, is essentially divided into four distinct regions. What is now known as the Borders was during the time of the Romans

densely wooded, and the Southern Uplands added to the obstacles faced by any military force moving into the area. The second area, the Lowlands, was crisscrossed by a number of major rivers, including the Clyde, the Forth and the Tay. These permanent geographical features made north-to-south travel especially problematic. The areas around the rivers were also marshy, making any building extra difficult and risky. The Highlands, as the region's name suggests, is mountainous, and travel was restricted to the few mountain passes through the glens. These glens were ideal places for ambushes, which is something the Romans learned the hard way.

What the above information suggests is that the Highlands can never be conquered in the face of tyranny. Tyrannies can come and go but nature will resist all the way.

Perhaps what I saw that day at the top of Meall Dhuin Croisg, holds real truth. I was being given access to the collective of our human psyche *through* walking.

Blossoming Hands

That sweet soft scent from an apple tree in bloom is a smell of profound amazement. The garden in which I am standing is not my own but was once a peasant's. It is not a garden of dreams but a garden from a single dream landscape. The apple tree, placed within this designed and ordered garden, has presented to me that the tree itself is from outside the garden; here is not exactly where it intrinsically belongs. The apple tree and I live in that dream – together. Not a place to escape but a place of real beauty. Hence in any dream, beauty can only be provoked from imagination. How can anyone ignore the beauty of nature? Yesterday, looking through a book of paintings by Van Gogh, I remembered *Blossoming Pear Tree*. I noticed that from a distance when looking at the painting, it gave the impression of church bells, petals jingling. It could be heard as well as seen. As though the image itself was vibrating before me, alive.

Then walking slowly, barefoot on the green grass, I notice the distance I have yet to travel before I arrive at the tree. I am surrounded by a creative atmosphere that continues to animate around this ethereal apple tree. Scents, colours, sunlight; the whole space creates a sense of harmony.

Standing now in front of the tree, its light has become intensified. I appear to be almost touching light. At every moment I feel as though I am dissolving, quietly forgetting myself and the world I was once in. Tiny flies and birds are flying almost everywhere. I can smell scents that have no name. Scent truly makes one appreciate the intricate moments that are in place in life for us to enjoy.

Then pulling my hand from out of my pocket, still enjoying the tickling blades of grass from beneath my feet, I start to reach out my arm to pull a small branch in flower towards me.

Whilst looking, I'm moving my entire body, arm, hand and then gently my fingers, as they begin to open and receive.

The apple flower is now touching my nose; its petals are tickling my nostrils. Then beginning to smell, I close my eye lids gently. In the act of smelling, we instinctively want to experience the isolation between our visual world and that of smell. In the act of closing our eyes, darkness creates a kind of forgetfulness – a moment's respite from looking. This moment of smelling and not looking creates our reciprocal approach between thought and feeling. We lapse into our senses. By isolating our senses in the mind, we begin to live within the sensations of our imagination. For many humans closing their eyes when in the act of smelling a flower has become a natural act. However, for some it is still an act of romanticism – because this is seen as being romantic, it cannot constitute reality; for them, it does not exist. Mystery is inexplicable. Once isolated, sensation becomes everything.

Breathing in slowly, through my nostrils and into my lungs, the scent of the flower is now present. I am now not only feeling the sensation of scent but I am experiencing it. The mind instantly tries to process and present to us – what is it I'm smelling? We can never name the smell, only describe it. Immediately at that point in which my eyes are closed, I am travelling, somewhere within, and yet outside myself. Where? I don't know. As though the flower's stigma has sucked me into an eternal and intimate space, a kind of sanctuary. I wish I could encapsulate this sweet scent, so that every time I sleep or awake I can experience the sensation that life is eternal again and again.

When in the act of smelling a flower, this fusion of scent and imagination represents the sensation that life is eternal, and also death.

And so, it appears,

that to die actually is a pleasant experience.

'The human mind cannot be absolutely destroyed with the human body, but something of it remains, which is eternal.' Baruch Spinoza, *Ethics*, Part V, Proposition XXIII.

Ben Lawers: The Ontology of a Mountain

How does a mountain contribute to the quality of your life? How can we measure its powerful ontological quality when walking? What significant moments are we searching for?

Every morning in front of a mountain are glimpses of the beginning, of creation.

Ben Lawers is flesh and spirit in *unity*. Her name translates as 'speaking mountain'.

As the weather began to change, the further up the mountain I went, so did my being, becoming more eternal, as I was surrounded by the eternal.

When we walk up a mountain, its shape is continuously changing and therefore our shape is too, giving us new perspectives, an aspect of the whole ontological experience of mountain walking. Up here, heaven, I realised, is the air we breathe.

From the village of Killin, Ben Lawers appears large (like a volcano). But when you are closer to the top, you realise that it seems to have shrunk. And then, when you reach the top, instead of being at the summit of Ben Lawers, you have arrived at a new space, an elsewhere. A new landscape has opened up. A new shape. You are elsewhere, because you have no name for this landscape. Having entered into this new space, it begins to open up your mind (imagination), and simultaneously expands upon your *being* in the world. Is this how one becomes the mountain one is seeing and now walking, at one with nature, fused?

Maybe it is not so important. Objects in nature that become smaller, become more intimate. The essence of nature more eminent, essential and therefore more deeply felt. Photographs can never do justice or justify the whole experience. Mountains have to be walked, climbed and through our efforts we are rewarded with a new ontological sphere, that we present to the world in our renewed presence. We have rediscovered new ontological maps of being in the world through mountain walking. Only one aspect of life in our ontological journey. All our dreams are still up there in the mountains. And as we return to ground zero, only then do we know a little more about life, ourselves and the universe.

Be Your Own Tour Guide: Rediscover Your Ontological Destiny

Inspiration: Make the *connection* between the presence of a tour guide, nature and yourself as your own ontological destiny of being in the world.

When we take someone on a tour, we are not just taking them to be in the presence of nature, we are also taking them on a tour through the *unique* presence of ourselves. We are very much part of the ethical experience. There is an essence within us waiting to be revealed and presented to the world. It is, fundamentally, a collaboration between us and nature and those we guide. Sense and enjoy the interaction ... what do you notice?

Our presence is not just a question of the image we seek to project but instead our *being* in the *here* and *now* with those we guide - an *eternal presence*. Presence is everything. Nature exemplifies this over and over, every day for us. Another example for self-practice, are we being courteous during a tour? Are we being patient? Are we talking too much? Are we allowing enough space to come into our tours? Are we remembering at all times that the tour is about those we guide and their place in nature?

Our aim should always be for a more loving presence towards ourselves and everyone around us. There, we will find something (and therefore a connection), as the beginning of your own ontological destiny.

Today the world is changing … and it's changing fast. But before you interpret the 'world is changing fast' as a prompt for fear, recognise that the world is in fact *returning* to something of a more intrinsic state, an essential planet to our being in the world. The point is this – rather than resisting, let us go with it. Rise to the challenge. *Be* bold. *Be* fearless. *Be* your essential and eternal self.

Beyond Ecotourism

Our ontological destiny is not about successful business transactions or the maximisation of profits, fundamentally instead in our daily exchanges (or gestures) we are looking for the opportunity to *propose* a new way of being in the world, which can only be achieved when you are being your essential self, the *eternal you*.

Everyday interactions with people are all contributing to your unique presence in the world, whether your experience of them is bad or good. Have faith.

For example, I often find myself taking a stranger on a tour without realising. I'm not looking for payment or an acknowledgment (I have already been rewarded). You see, the *more* we improve the experience of life for another, the greater the world will become today and tomorrow. Never underestimate your own power not only in the here and now but within your own community; therefore, improving social proximity.

Furthermore, our ontological destiny isn't only or always defined by human relationships. It can also be realised through our connection with nature. Once again, we spread like a sower the essence of our being around us, each day and every day. Notice how this will improve an intimate relationship, friendships and family interaction. Let us bring back the sacred into our everyday interactions and connections with other people (not only when we are guiding others on a tour).

What will my ontological destiny lead me to? Ontological *unity* – the very reason we are here and want to *be*.

And if we want to go further, we should make it our daily focus for everyone else to achieve their unity too. This, of course, is the journey of life – it doesn't happen overnight. Therefore, let our ontological destiny be the focus of our being. We should try each day to become our unique, essential and eternal selves in the world. Once achieved, notice how more and more of our eternal self is revealed, becoming an ever greater and more powerful presence.

Remember . . .

Destiny is in our *being*, presence.

Let that be our new daily focus...

Eternal Mountain (Meall nan Tarmachan and Ben Lawers)

The freshness of my arrival in this mountain village, the eternal appearances of nature all surrounding me was and still is life enhancing – a real presence. To this day, I will never forget how the moon one evening during my first summer felt so close that it had somehow rekindled something of a deep memory from my childhood; the sight itself *returned* me in a healing way. The moon and the sky that evening became the perfect holding environment. The moon, like the stars, is an essential part of the divine child within us all – our being. Eternal sky. Eternal moon. Eternal stars. Eternal universe. Eternal me. Eternal you. Eternal child.

> Eternal mountain
> Slabs of rock or shaped?

> Draw the horizon looking up towards the mountain, amidst the trees and sunlight. As I look up towards the outline of the mountain, and see the sunlight beaming across its surface into my eyes; from what I am seeing, it makes me feel as though such a golden light is at the palm of my hand, and that strangely I can paint with this light for waking dreams. Maybe, connect this sloping hill (with a drawing) of the mountain in Scotland to the eternal Matsutake story with regards to the Japanese word *Satoyama* - A border zone or area between mountain foothills and arable flat land in Japan.

> This coming spring, I find myself amongst mountains, a spring mountain. I feel myself for a moment to be in Syria. Searching for the light they are now searching in a time of crisis.

Wherever I go, we take our shared imagination with us and in this place, I have to connect with all that needs to be.

I don't want to be cremated; I want my bones to be settled upon the surface of the Earth.

Mountains open up new worlds.

Today's mountains stripped of their intrinsic foliage seem empty and bare. Nothing is moving except the sky above you. Real mountains should continuously be *moving*. Pulsating in our every step as we get closer to their pumping blood.

Everywhere upon this mountain valley are *small sacred places*.

In between the sloping hills of the mountains are isolated moss-covered trees, small streams and with their sound, I arrive immediately into a sanctuary.

Living amongst the mountains, one feels eternal every day.

I begin to notice the sheep's manure and immediately as I looked ahead of me, I began to see their labyrinth of tiny paths, leading you where?

Every layer of mist reveals a new mountain - unforeseen.

When you look at Ben Lawers from the village, one feels a kind of relationship forming. Mountains stand still and yet they move too. Quietly they grab your attention, there is no getting away. What is this relationship I am attempting to describe?

In the winter when it snows, when each snowflake is gently laid upon on the mountains, their peaks become soft pillows, with each second passing you're watching is comforted with the hope of what life can be.

The sight of a full arched rainbow before a mountain is always a reminder of life as a miracle. In the future, people will run out from their homes and stay until such a sight has once again disappeared, returning when a rainbow reappears.

The flesh of God is all around us, every leaf and petal. Every scent his breath.

Mountains teach you silence. Go and sit with them.

Trees sometimes are like musical conductors, their every branch reaching out and up towards the sky; composing music for us to hear - the rhythm of our Earth.

What I love most about mountains is their presence. They offer you a blanket, a pillow on which to lay your head and shield you from the wind. They above all else, offer us hope on life's journey.

Arriving at the eternal has a lot to do with the way clouds move, continuously eternal in form and expression. The way they are formed is a kind of *convergence*.

We are surrounded by the eternal expressions of nature.

Everything in nature has come into an eternal presence.

Mountains live without time.

I could spend an eternity just looking at rocks.

A cow's "moo" echoes across the glen, bouncing from one mountain to another and is returned back to the cow: each time the cow is made aware of its existence.

There is always something quite sacred and organic about the ground on which cows have walked, their pasture is laden with rocks and tree branches, their soil subtle, moist, and soft. Growing a new grass, a brighter green.

Mountain Landscape in Spring

Spring represents the joy of that *thread* between pleasure and pain, a unity of the two which is happiness. For both must be *living* and present as a reminder, not of consequence but of what one has overcome.

A thread of pain. This is necessary to the principal of eternity.

It is the direction in which the thread of spring stems that is significant – its travelling force felt silently. It's about how spring enters you. Spring is the thread and the needle is like a breeze that stretches across our landscapes.

Walking beside a farm hedge: Birds are flying past me. Then I thought...What if evolution worked in the *opposite* direction? By that direction I'm not talking about the biological aspect of life but the spiritual. I'll make it clearer, what if the final, or rather eternal destination of the human spirit is that of becoming a bird?

Rediscovered the Lady's Hem (a flower).

Wilderness is the origin of our waking dreams.

Woodland Garden (Ben Lawers)

Downy birch…what beautiful skin they have.

Woodlands are intimate spaces.

What disappears when climbing a mountain, or rather gives us clues to what will? Erosion I think is the most basic of clues to an eventual disappearance and how soon it will disappear, creating new mountains.

Stream Gypsy (Meall nan Tarmachan)

Walking down from the ridge by a rocky stream, a Dipper greeted me. They fly with intense speed. As she landed on a rock she hopped and danced. For Dippers, the celebration is water. By greeting me she was letting me know that she was here, that she exists and through my presence I confirmed and shared with her that celebration and importantly her own expression of gratitude for being. I went a little closer to her and then she took off like a shooting star, up the stream and round the bend. After a minute I wondered, where did she come from? Then I saw a rock in the stream wearing her gauntlet made of purple saxifrage, it was from the flower she came. What will she become now? I don't know. I must follow her.

As I go into the stream, I feel myself going into the ridge of the mountain, the earth itself. Beside a small waterfall, I see bronze or brown *algae* like a butterfly. In the rock I saw the imprint or the printed colours of a butterfly, as though she had pressed herself against the rock beneath the waterfall. Everything was coming out, out from the rocks.

Bonsai is everywhere in this landscape. I am somewhere in Japan or China amongst the Yellow Mountains.

Water is the symbol of transcendence.

I looked up at the sky one day and saw the patterned clouds in the shape of the stream's bed – *dunes*. In stream morphology: a dune is 'a hill or ridge of sand piled up by the wind.' The fluvial processes are in the sky?

On the ground before you, you saw nothing, then the earth moved, and you saw everything, seeing two baby birds at your feet. This is what I saw one day, during one summer in Killin.

Stream Morphology

Then there is the *overall* energy of the stream.
Sediments to make new lands, therefore new worlds.
Sediment and flourishment.
Time of the river? Is eternal.

Mountains in Autumn (Loch Tay)

From the loch came the frog. From the frog came the bat.

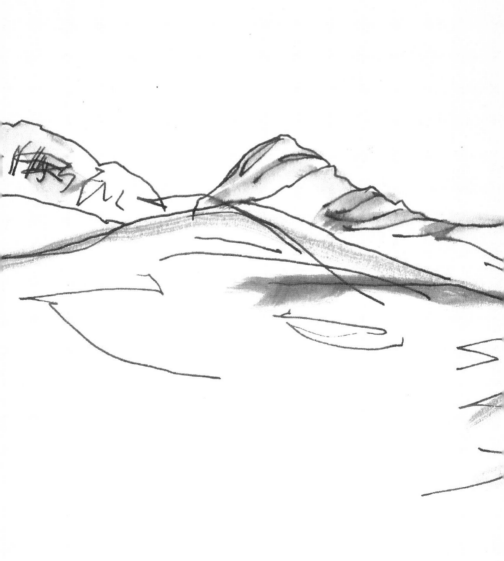

Postscript: Nature First

Eternal Mountain is about more than a historical tour guide in Breadalbane, rather from a sustainable-perspective, I put nature first at the heart of our local economy today.

Therefore, I see being an eco-tour guide as the beginning of that process and as a way to inspire others. Bringing together history, people from all over the world that come to visit and most essentially in the realisation of their part in nature too. It is also about having a renewed appreciation of nature, rather than the dogmatic perspective of seeing nature at 'our disposal' and as a way to exploit; serving only our needs. Crucially, it is also about remembering that nature supports all forms of life, each life being essential to the other. And, importantly, recognising that the climate crisis is not going to go away – it will remain an issue for some time, until we take real action.

Being an eco-tour guide is therefore in many ways an ethical statement, not just about putting nature first, but also about the opportunity to create ethical job roles within our communities, that are low-carbon and therefore less damaging to our planet. This, I believe, is the future of humanity if we are really going to survive and it represents the serious need for a universal basic income for everyone, who like myself, living in a rural and remote location, does not have a monopoly in today's markets. Neo-liberalism has no place in a village, representing instead social inequality and collapse for nature. Eco-tourism therefore is a way of embracing the challenge of today's human ontological crisis. If we are prepared to put nature first at the heart of our local economy, we can contribute to our well-being and that of visitors. Overall, I offer a rich and deep experience of nature. Only our local history can truly ground us, keeping the human imagination alive and well, helping us to look towards a future with continued and renewed hope.

https://www.eternalmountaintourguide.co.uk/https-www-eternalmountaintourguide-1

PRIVATE TOURS

Breadalbane – Home of Giants

Private Village Tour - Morning / Afternoon

£99 for 2 people - 2 Hours (approx)

Looking to experience breath-taking scenery with a local viewpoint? If you are, then this short tour is the best option for you. Let me take care of you, as we take a journey from the Stone Circle of Killin, to embrace the powerful energy of Dochart Falls, visit a former meal mill, founded by the Irish, Gaelic-speaking priest St Fillan, stroll to Fingal's Stone, the burial-place of Fionn Mac Cumhaill, the great warrior from Celtic mythology. Then explore the ruins of Finlarig Castle and finally to the resting nest of Loch Tay, where we shall learn of the folkloric tale of its origin.

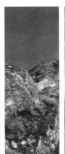

Eternal Mountain – *Essays from Afar*

First published June 2021.

Expressive Press
Killin,
Stirling
Scotland.

British Library Cataloguing In Publication Data.

Paperback: ISBN 978-1-8384247-3-2
eBook: ISBN 978-1-8384247-4-9

References & Acknowledgments

Patrick Phillips: cover images and all other page images © Patrick Phillips, accept pages 38, 39, 40 and 41.

Page 10, 'The point about centre...' John Berger interview from the documentary film *A Kind of Grace.* Transmission date unknown. *https://www.youtube.com/watch?v=JzcQUPnm3Z0&t=1878s*

Page 12, *Breadalbane: Home of Giants* first published in The Voice – The magazine of the Friends of Loch Lomond and the Trossachs. Spring/Summer 2020 | No. 25. https://www.lochlomondtrossachs.org.uk/the-voice

Page 13, *Forgotten Village Of Tirai (Glen Lochay)* factual narratives and historical dates quoted from *Tirai and Easter Tullich - An Archaeological Field Survey in Glen Lochay* Edited by Dugald MacInnes Anne Wood and J Scott Wood Including *A Summary of Geology and Soils* by Roland Golightly. Association of Certificated Field Archaeologists Occasional Paper Number 126, 2014. ISBN 978-0-9574600-6-5. Further information can be obtained from the ACFA website: www.acfabaseline.info

Page 38 *Wildlife Photographer – Richard Phillips* Copyright © Richard Phillips: photographs.

Page 42, *Rediscover Your Connection With Nature Through Ecotourism* first published in The Perthshire Magazine – March 2020. https://www.theperthshiremagazine.com/current-issue Also, *The International Ecotourism Society* 2015 definition for 'ecotourism' can be found at https://ecotourism.org/what-is-ecotourism/

Page 46, *Climate Change: Creativity & Survival* first published in SceneStirling – September 2020.
https://scenestirling.com/blog/climateandcreativity. Also, the quote from the TV interview with John Berger *'This creativity, which we are so attracted by in artists....'* Transmission Sat 13th Jun 1970, 22:40 on BBC Two England. *John Berger Talks to James Mossman* from *The Weekly Arts Magazine* programme. 'John Berger, art critic and novelist, talks to James Mossman about the future of painting.' Below is a short clip, full interview cannot be found online.
https://www.youtube.com/watch?v=6s5F0Wl3gnc

Page 61, *Blossoming Hands* first published in Elsewhere Journal – January 2017.
https://www.elsewherejournal.com/blog/2017/1/29/blossoming-hands

Page 76, *Be Your Own Tour Guide: Rediscover Your Ontological Destiny*. I would like to thank David Richo, PhD, MFT, a psychotherapist, teacher, workshop leader, and writer who works in Santa Barbara and San Francisco California for his inspiration to write this article.
https://davericho.com/

About the Author: Eternal revolutionary, writer and artist Patrick Phillips was born in Cornwall in 1984. He lives and works in a mountain village in Scotland. He has written articles for *The Stage*, *Elsewhere Journal*, *CommonSpace*, *Scottish Left Review*, *Freedom Press*, *Scottish Farmer* and *The National*. This is his second non-fiction book. His latest project *The Modern Giant*, will look closer at today's human ontological crisis with a new perspective - it will be published in 2023. https://www.patrickphillips.online/

Printed in Great Britain
by Amazon

64530196R00054